Egg Fried Rice

Written by Roderick Hunt

Illustrated by Nick Schon,
based on the original characters
created by Alex Brychta

Read these words

fried

rice

tried

nine

cried

invite

nice

smiled

“I will be nine on Friday,” said Wilma. “I’d like to eat out.”

"I'd like a Chinese meal," Wilma said, "and can we invite Biff and Chip?"

“That’s fine,” said Mum.

It was time for the Chinese meal.
They went to the Bright Sky.

“What is it like to be nine?” said Chip. Wilma smiled.

“It’s all right,” she said.

“What do you like best?” said Dad.

"I like egg fried rice," said Wilma, "and I'll try tiger prawns."

Then all the lights went out.
Oh no. There was a fire.

“The kitchen is on fire,” said Mr Lee.

They had to go outside.
Fire-fighters came to put the fire out.

"I am sorry," said Mr Lee.
"We must shut for the night."

Wilma was upset. She tried not to, but she cried.

“It is sad to see Wilma cry,” said Mr Lee. “Come back on Sunday night.”

On Sunday, Mr Lee put on a feast.

"Smile," said Mr Lee.

"This is so kind," said Mum.

"I had my egg fried rice," said Wilma, "and such a nice time."

Talk about the story

Where did the family go for their meal?

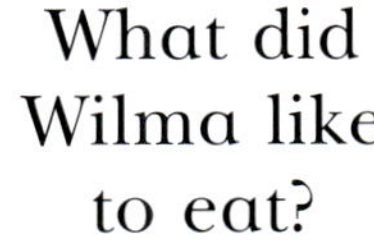

What did Wilma like to eat?

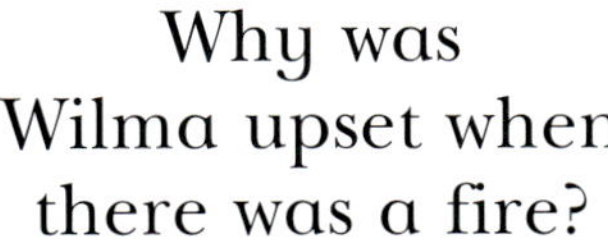

Why was Wilma upset when there was a fire?

What do you like to eat when you go out for a meal?

ie, *i-e* or *igh*?

Choose the letters to make each word.

n____t	n_n_	sm_l_
tr____d	l_k_	r____t
br____t	fr____d	t_m_